TECHNICAL PRESENTATION SKILLS

Revised Edition

Steve Mandel

A FIFTY-MINUTE™ SERIES BOOK

CRISP PUBLICATIONS, INC.
Menlo Park, California

TECHNICAL PRESENTATION SKILLS

Revised Edition

Steve Mandel

CREDITS
Editor: **Michael G. Crisp**
Layout & Composition: **Interface Studio**
Cover Design: **Carol Harris**
Artwork: **Ralph Mapson**

Copyright © 1988, 1994 by Steve Mandel
Printed in the United States of America

Distribution to the U.S. Trade:

National Book Network, Inc.
4720 Boston Way
Lanham, MD 20706
1-800-462-6420

Library of Congress Catalog Card Number 93-074052
Mandel, Steve
Technical Presentation Skills
ISBN 1-56052-263-1

This book is printed on recyclable paper with soy ink.

PREFACE

The study of how to give effective speeches dates back to ancient Greece. Around 350 B.C. Aristotle wrote his famous *Rhetoric*, now considered to be one of the first formal books on the subject. Now 2,300 years later, we are still struggling with the same problems the Greeks encountered and that speakers have struggled with throughout the ages.

The advent of technology has both complicated and simplified the task of the speaker. For example, today it is possible to produce complex graphs on a computer that will, in turn, produce overhead transparencies. But how much information should we put on that graph? And, most important, where does that graph fit into the organizational plan of the presentation.

Technical Presentation Skills attempts to answer the fundamental questions of how to prepare and deliver technical material effectively. Proven techniques are presented that will give a reader the necessary skills to give more confident, enthusiastic and persuasive presentations. Topics such as: how to use body language effectively; how to organize thoughts and data for maximum impact; how to develop and use visual aids, as well as (of course) how to deliver what you have prepared. The problem of delivering a technical paper at a professional meeting is also covered.

This book provides some theory but more often presents simple and practical suggestions on how to give more effective technical presentations.

ABOUT THIS BOOK

TECHNICAL PRESENTATION SKILLS is not like most books. It has a unique ''self-paced'' format that encourages a reader to become personally involved. Designed to be ''read with a pencil,'' there are abundant exercises, activities, assessments and cases that invite participation.

The objective of this book is to help a person organize, plan, and deliver an effective presentation to others.

THIS BOOK (and the other self-improvement titles listed in the back of the book) can be used effectively in a number of ways. Here are some possibilities:

—**Individual Study.** Because the book is self-instructional, all that is needed is a quiet place, some time and a pencil. Completing the activities and exercises will provide valuable feedback, as well as practical ideas for self-improvement.

—**Workshops and Seminars.** This book is ideal for use during, or as pre-assigned reading prior to a workshop or seminar. With the basics in hand, the quality of participation will improve. More time can be spent practicing concept extensions and applications during the program.

—**College Programs.** Thanks to the format, brevity and low cost, this book is ideal for short courses and extension programs.

There are other possibilities that depend on the objectives of the user. One thing for sure, even after it has been read, this book will serve as excellent reference material which can be easily reviewed.

DEDICATION

This book is dedicated to those who helped make it happen and without whose support it would not exist: my wonderful wife Carol, my kids Joe, Paul and Alex, my colleague Kathleen Brown and all the folks at Crisp Publications.

For more information:

A two-day workshop based on the material in this book and the author's other Fifty-Minute book, *Effective Presentation Skills*, is available from Mandel Communications. Please contact us for more information at:

Mandel Communications
1425 Hidden Valley Road
Soquel, CA 95073

1-800-262-6335

TO THE READER

There is a myth that great speakers are born, ''not made,'' that somehow certain individuals have the innate ability to stand in front of an audience with no anxiety, and give a moving, dynamic speech. Well, that just isn't so!

People we consider great speakers usually have spent years developing and practicing their skill. They had to start at the beginning and learn the basics of organization, preparation, delivery and dealing with anxiety. Once the basics were in hand they had to continue to build their abilities.

Professional athletes constantly practice the basics because they know that without such practice they will not survive. To an outsider, the thought of a professional golfer (for example) spending hour upon hour practicing the basics may seem ridiculous. But to that professional, the mastery of those basic skills are the very foundation of success.

Learning to be a better speaker is similar to learning any activity. In the beginning it can be frustrating. After a few lessons where you learn some theory and practice some of the basic skills, things usually improve. To really learn to do anything well takes constant practice and a mastery of the basics.

Speaking is no different. Before becoming comfortable as a speaker you need to learn some basic skills and then actively seek places to practice those skills. This may mean walking into your manager's office and volunteering to give more presentations, or joining a speaking club which allows you to speak in an organized setting. The more experience you gain, the more proficient and comfortable you will become.

Good luck!
Steve Mandel

DEFINITIONS

The terms ''speech'' and ''technical presentation'' are often used interchangeably. For our purposes it is useful to understand the difference.

A technical presentation is a specialized type of speech. Typically, when we think of a speech we think of a dedication speech, a political speech, a speech of tribute or some similar event that is more public in nature than a presentation would be.

Technical presentations are speeches that are usually given in a business, financial, technical, professional or scientific environment and usually involve the discussion of data. The audience is likely to be more specialized than those attending a typical speech event.

Although the difference between speeches and presentations is slight, this book leans toward helping those who give technical presentations. But, because a presentation is a type of speech, there are ideas and skills in this book that will also be helpful to any speech-maker.

CONTENTS

CONTENTS

CONTENTS (Continued)

P A R T

I

ASSESSING YOUR SKILLS

EVALUATE YOURSELF

Check the category that best describes you as a speaker:

Category	Characteristics
_____ **AVOIDER**	An avoider does everything possible to escape from having to get in front of an audience. In some cases avoiders may seek careers that do not involve making presentations.
_____ **RESISTER**	A resister has fear when asked to speak. This fear may be strong. Resisters may not be able to avoid speaking as part of their job, but they never encourage it. When they do speak they do so with great reluctance and considerable pain.
_____ **ACCEPTER**	The accepter will give presentations as part of the job but doesn't seek those opportunities. Accepters occasionally give a presentation and feel like they did a good job. They even find that once in a while they are quite persuasive, and enjoy speaking in front of a group.
_____ **SEEKER**	A seeker looks for opportunities to speak. The seeker understands that anxiety can be a stimulant which fuels enthusiasm during a presentation. Seekers work at building their professional communication skills and self-confidence by speaking often.

PRESENT PRESENTATION SKILLS SELF-EVALUATION

To be a more effective presenter it is useful to examine your present skills. The following evaluation can help determine the areas on which to focus to increase your competency. Please read the statement and then circle the number that best describes you. Then concentrate during the balance of this book on those items you marked 1, 2 or 3.

	Always				Never

1. I determine some basic objectives before planning a presentation. 5 4 3 2 1

2. I analyze the values, needs and constraints of my audience. 5 4 3 2 1

3. I write down some main ideas first, in order to build a presentation around them. 5 4 3 2 1

4. I incorporate both a preview and review of the main ideas as my presentation is organized. 5 4 3 2 1

5. I develop an introduction that will catch the attention of my audience and still provide the necessary background information. 5 4 3 2 1

6. My conclusion refers back to the introduction and, if appropriate, contains a call-to-action statement. 5 4 3 2 1

7. The visual aids I use are carefully prepared, simple, easy to read, and have impact. 5 4 3 2 1

8. The number of visual aids will enhance, not detract, from my presentation. 5 4 3 2 1

9. If my presentation is persuasive, arguments are used that are logical and that support my assertions. 5 4 3 2 1

10. I use anxiety to fuel the enthusiasm of my presentation, not hold me back. 5 4 3 2 1

11. I insure the benefits suggested to my audience are clear and compelling. 5 4 3 2 1

12. I communicate ideas with enthusiasm. 5 4 3 2 1

13. I rehearsed so there is a minimum focus on notes and maximum attention paid to my audience. 5 4 3 2 1

	Always				Never

14. My notes contain only "key words" so I avoid reading from a manuscript or technical paper.   5 4 3 2 1

15. My presentations are rehearsed standing up and using visual aids.   5 4 3 2 1

16. I prepare answers to anticipated questions, and practice responding to them.   5 4 3 2 1

17. I arrange seating (if appropriate) and check audio-visual equipment in advance of the presentation.   5 4 3 2 1

18. I maintain good eye contact with the audience at all times.   5 4 3 2 1

19. My gestures are natural and not constrained by anxiety.   5 4 3 2 1

20. My voice is strong and clear and is not a monotone.   5 4 3 2 1

Total score _____

If you scored between 80-100, you are an accomplished speaker who simply needs to maintain basic skills through practice.

If your total score was between 60-80, you have the potential to become a highly effective presenter.

If your score was between 40 and 60, this book can help you significantly.

If you scored between 30 and 40, you should show dramatic improvement with practice.

If your total was below 30, roll up your sleeves and dig in. It may not be easy- but you can make excellent progress if you try.

At the conclusion of this program, take this evaluation again and compare your scores. You should be pleased with the progress you have made.

Technical Presentation Skills

SET SOME GOALS

If your score on the previous page was:

90–100   You have the qualities of an excellent presenter.

70–89   You are above average but could improve in some areas.

Below 69   This program should help you.

WHAT GOALS DO YOU WANT TO ACHIEVE?

Using the information from the self-evaluation form on pages 4 and 5, check those boxes that indicate goals that you would like to achieve:

I hope to:

☐ understand the anxiety I feel before a presentation and learn how to use it constructively during my presentation.

☐ learn how to organize my thoughts and data in a logical and concise manner.

☐ develop the necessary skills to communicate enthusiasm about the ideas I present, and develop a more dynamic presentation style.

☐ transform question and answer sessions into an enjoyable and productive part of the presentation process.

☐ construct visual aids that have impact, and use them effectively during my presentation.

☐ make even the most technical presentation a lively and interesting event.

DEALING WITH ANXIETY

Anxiety is a natural state that exists any time we are placed under stress. Giving a presentation normally will cause some stress. When this type of stress occurs, physiological changes take place that may cause symptoms such as a nervous stomach, sweating, tremors in the hands and legs, accelerated breathing, and/or increased heart rate.

Don't worry! If you have any of these symptoms before or during a presentation you are normal. If none of these things happen you are one in a million. Almost everyone experiences some stress before presentations, even when the task is something simple like, ''tell the group something about yourself.'' The trick is to make your excess energy work for you.

When you learn to make stress work for you, it can be the fuel for a more enthusiastic and dynamic presentation. The next few pages will teach you how to recycle your stress in a positive form that will help you become a better presenter.

As someone once said, **''the trick is to get those butterflies in your stomach to all fly in one direction!''**

DEALING WITH ANXIETY (Continued)

> **Leo** is an engineer with an electronics firm. In two weeks he has to deliver a major presentation to managers from several divisions, on a project he is proposing. He knows his topic, but his audience will be examining his proposal very closely, and Leo is certain he will receive some very tough questions. Every time Leo thinks about planning what to say, he gets too nervous to begin work.

If Leo's problem of anxiety before a presentation sounds familiar then the following may help:

TIPS FOR REDUCING ANXIETY

1. *ORGANIZE*

Lack of organization is one of the major causes of anxiety. Later in this book you will learn a simple technique for organizing your presentation. Knowing that your thoughts are well organized will give you more confidence, which will allow you to focus energy into your presentation.

2. *VISUALIZE*

Imagine walking into a room, being introduced, delivering your presentation with enthusiasm, fielding questions with confidence and leaving the room knowing you did a great job. Mentally rehearse this sequence with all the details of your particular situation, and it will help you focus on what you need to do to be successful.

3. *PRACTICE*

Many speakers rehearse a presentation mentally or with just their lips. Instead, you should practice standing up, as if an audience were in front of you, and use your visual aids (if you have them). At least two dress rehearsals are recommended. If possible, have somebody critique the first one and/or have it videotaped. Watch the playback, listen to the critique and incorporate any changes you feel are required before your final practice session. *There is no better preparation than this.*

> Carol is an account executive with a software company. She has been asked to present the sales figures for her region at the company's national sales meeting. Her colleague Jack is finishing his remarks and in two minutes she will have to stand up and make her presentation. She is experiencing extreme anxiety at a time when she needs to be focused and collected.

Carol's situation is quite common. If you experience anxiety immediately before speaking, try some of the following exercises next time you're waiting for your turn to stand up and speak:

4. *BREATHE*

When your muscles tighten and you feel nervous, you may not be breathing deeply enough. The first thing to do is to sit up, erect but relaxed, and inhale deeply a number of times.

5. *FOCUS ON RELAXING*

Instead of thinking about the tension—focus on relaxing. As you breathe, tell yourself on the inhale, "I am" and on the exhale, "relaxed." Try to clear your mind of everything except the repetition of the "I am-relaxed" statement and continue this exercise for several minutes.

6. *RELEASE TENSION*

As tension increases and your muscles tighten, nervous energy can get locked into the limbs. This unreleased energy may cause your hands and legs to shake. Before standing up to give a presentation, it is a good idea to try to release some of this pent up tension by doing a simple, unobtrusive isometric exercise.

Starting with your toes and calf muscles, tighten your muscles up through your body finally making a fist (i.e. toes, feet, calves, thighs, stomach, chest, shoulders, arms and fingers). Immediately release all of the tension and take a deep breath. Repeat this exercise until you feel the tension start to drain away. Remember, this exercise is to be done quietly so that no one knows you're relaxing!

DEALING WITH ANXIETY (Continued)

> **Andrew** is a chemist with a major pharmaceutical company. When he gives presentations he gets very nervous. He sweats, his hands tremble, his voice becomes a monotone (and at times inaudible). He also fidgets with items, such as a pen, and looks at his notes or the overhead projector screen, not at his audience. He can barely wait to finish and return to his seat.

Andrew's plight is not uncommon. You may not have all of these symptoms but you can probably relate to some of them. The following techniques will help you in situations where you get nervous while speaking.

7. *MOVE*

Speakers who stand in one spot and never gesture experience tension. In order to relax you need to release tension by allowing your muscles to flex. If you find you are locking your arms in one position when you speak, then practice releasing them so that they do the same thing they would if you were in an animated one-on-one conversation. You can't gesture too much if it is natural.

Upper body movement is important, but moving with your feet can serve to release tension as well. You should be able to take a few steps, either side-to-side or toward the audience. When speaking from a lectern you can move around the side of it for emphasis (if you have a moveable microphone). This movement will help release your tension and never fails to draw the audience into the presentation. If you can't move to the side of the lectern, an occasional half-step to one side will help loosen muscle tension.

8. *EYE CONTACT WITH THE AUDIENCE*

Try to make your presentation similar to a one-on-one conversation. Relate with your audience as individuals. Look in peoples' eyes as you speak. Connect with them. Make it personal and personable. The eye contact should help you relax because you become less isolated from the audience, and learn to react to their interest in you.

SECTION REVIEW—DEALING WITH ANXIETY CHECKLIST

Check those items which you intend to practice and incorporate in the future presentations you make.

I plan to:

☐ organize my material.

☐ visualize myself delivering a successful presentation.

☐ rehearse by standing up and using all of my visual aids.

☐ breathe deeply just prior to speaking.

☐ focus on relaxing with simple, unobtrusive isometric techniques.

☐ release my tension in a positive way by directing it to my audience.

☐ move when I speak to stay relaxed and natural.

☐ maintain good eye contact with my audience.

PRACTICE MAKES PERFECT

P A R T

II

PLANNING YOUR PRESENTATION

PERSONAL APPEARANCE

Personal Appearance in a Presentation

This chapter is not intended to provide specific fashion guidelines but rather some general considerations on your dress and appearance. In general, avoid excess. Keep patterns, accessories and colors simple. You should be the focus, not what you're wearing.

For Women

1. Clothes should fit well, not too tight. Hemline length should be decided upon by what works for you and *what you will look like to those in the audience,* especially if you are sitting up on a stage. Generally, longer sleeves are recommended to maintain a more businesslike appearance.

2. Find two or three colors that work well with your complexion and hair color. You might wish to consult one of the many books on the subject or contact a ''color consultant.'' You can then combine complimentary accessories with your basic outfits to provide variety. Find good fabrics and make sure that they don't make noise when you move! Generally, avoid very bright reds and oranges and blacks and whites since these colors are harsher and tend to draw attention away from the face.

3. Avoid jewelry that sparkles, dangles or makes noise. Subtle accessories are more appropriate when you are the presenter. Earrings, broaches and bracelets that distract will annoy the audience and draw attention away from your presentation.

4. Makeup should be simple and compliment the wearer. Overdone makeup can become the focus of negative, and unwanted, attention. Makeup that is well done can control oily areas of the face that might reflect light, enhance natural features and help you look more relaxed even in the most difficult presentation situations.

5. Hair, like other aspects of our appearance, should add to a positive overall impression of our appearance. While styles are highly individual they should not be the dominate feature of the face. Hair that falls below about 1/2 inch above the eyebrow seriously interferes with the audience's ability to read your face since a lot of information is communicated from this area.

PERSONAL APPEARANCE (Continued)

For Men

1. Suits should be well tailored. For presentations, clothes that are checkered, brightly colored or that clash will not reflect well on your image. Generally, dark blues, greys and blacks in single or double-breasted classic styles are the safest bet. Depending on the audience, a sport coat and well matched trousers are acceptable.

2. Men's suit coats are designed to be buttoned whereas most women's coats are not. In a presentation, depending on the level of formality, you may wish to button the jacket, unbutton it or take the coat off altogether.

3. Shirts should fit well and the collar should not be too tight. If you are worried about perspiration, make sure and wear a cotton T-shirt. If going on TV, avoid white shirts. The very best color is a light grey.

4. Ties can be used to compliment the color of your eyes and face. The traditional red ''power tie'' may not be the best color for you. Experiment a bit. The red tie causes the audience's eyes to focus first on the tie and not on you. Subtler colors may work better for you.

5. Shoes should be appropriate, comfortable and well-shined. Make sure that socks match, don't attract attention, and that they cover bare leg when you sit down.

6. Hair frames the face. It should be well-groomed regardless of style. Beards and mustaches should be well-groomed especially around the lip line. If you are bald, avoid bringing a long lock of hair across the head to try to cover the baldness—it only attracts more attention to the fact that you are bald. Learn to accept it. If you are afraid of the shine under lights, apply a little powder to the head. The powder can't be seen and it will cut down on the reflection.

And a word about glasses for both sexes . . .

The rule of thumb in presentations is to wear glasses if you need them to see the audience or read visual aids, etc. If you don't need them to see, or you can wear contacts, leave the glasses off. The reason for this is that the glass will reflect light in the room and the audience won't be able to see your eyes. Also, avoid tinted lenses since this will increase the audience's difficulty in seeing your eyes. There is an antireflective coating that is available that eliminates reflection and glare—it is highly recommended for presenters.

PLANNING YOUR PRESENTATION

Part of planning a presentation means that you must ask yourself why, not what. The "what" part will be answered when you begin to organize your thoughts. In the beginning you should concern yourself with *why* you are giving a presentation to a particular audience. The answer to this question should help you plan your presentation.

For example, you have been asked to give a presentation to a group of managers in your company on next year's departmental budget. Don't start writing down what you expect to say. Instead, ask yourself what you want to accomplish with your presentation. Will you be asking for a budget increase, or presenting a plan showing how you can operate on less money? Think about your specific objectives in relation to your audience before preparing your presentation.

STEP 1 - Develop Objectives

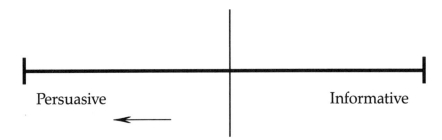

The P-I Diagram

This diagram describes the relationship between Persuasive and Informative presentations. They are not separate types but rather exist on a continuum. An example of an informative presentation at the far end of the diagram would be a status report or a project update. All persuasive presentations contain elements of information giving and all informative presentations contain elements of persuasion (although they may be very subtle, i.e. I want everyone to feel that I am knowledgeable on this topic.)

Heading in the direction of the arrow, presentations become more and more persuasive. When the vertical line in the center is crossed, in the direction of the arrow, the speaker tells the audience what change is requested; this in part, is the definition of a persuasive presentation. Presentations on the Informative side of the line *imply* that some action should be taken, in a stronger and stronger manner, as the center line is approached.

Using the P-I Diagram:

To help determine your objective, mark the place on the diagram where your presentation falls. Is it persuasive or informative?

ANALYZING YOUR AUDIENCE

When analyzing your audience you have four items to consider:

1. Values—What is important to the group? Different organizations have different value systems. Giving a presentation outside your organization is probably very different from presenting internally. Even different departments within an organization can have different values.

2. Needs—It is important to find out in advance of the presentation what the group thinks they need; this may be quite different from what you thought they needed. The speaker then must find a way to resolve the discrepancy.

3. Constraints—These are things that might hold the audience back from doing what you want them to do or from knowing what you want them to know. They include the following areas:

   A. Political: Internal politics can be a constraint. If you must get support from competing factions you must take that into consideration when organizing your presentation. In addition, personality clashes and other forms of conflict may interfere with your success.

   B. Financial: Whenever you ask for anything that is going to cost money you will encounter resistance. You must factor this resistance into your presentation and find ways to overcome it.

   C. Knowledge: All of us have our own area of specialization. We must be careful not to use technical language, abbreviations, acronyms, buzz words, etc., that people in the audience might not understand. If in doubt, ask the audience if they are familiar with the terminology and define it if necessary.

4. Demographic Information—Things like the size of the audience, location of the presentation, etc., may also influence the organization.

AUDIENCE ANALYSIS WORKSHEET

This form should help you plan more efficiently for any presentation.

1. My objectives in relation to my audience are:

    _____

2. Values that need to be considered with this particular audience include:

    _____

3. Constraints that must be recognized when speaking to this particular audience.

    _____

4. Special needs of this particular audience:

    _____

5. I would rate my audience's knowledge of the topic and technical terminology to be:

    High _____   Low _____   Mixed _____   Unknown _____

6. My assessment of the audience's willingness to accept the ideas I present is:

    High _____   Low _____   Mixed _____   Unknown _____

7. My audience has an opinion of me, as a speaker, prior to the presentation of:

    Good _____   Poor _____   Mixed _____   Unknown _____

8. Examples of supporting ideas and arguments likely to work well:

    _____

9. Examples of supporting ideas and arguments likely to cause a negative reaction_____

10. Audience Size _____   11. Length of Presentation _____

ORGANIZING YOUR PRESENTATION

This section will provide several steps which will assist you in organizing your thoughts for all future presentations. You will probably want to refer to this section of *Technical Presentation Skills* prior to your next several speaking assignments.

ORGANIZING YOUR THOUGHTS

It is always a good idea to start organizing the body of the speech and not worry about the introduction until later. Introductions are often generated by what goes into the body. Effective speakers have learned to build from the center of their speech outward. Following are some suggestions that might help you:

STEP #1 - Brainstorm Main Ideas

Using Post-It Notes* or a similar medium, brainstorm some possible main ideas for your presentation. Write one idea on each card. Let the ideas flow at this point, don't edit, (that will come later). The strategy is to generate as many ideas as possible.

Once you have a large number of ideas, begin eliminating. Try to end up with between two and five main ideas. This is a typical number for a presentation. If you have more than five ideas you should reduce them by making some of them subpoints.

EXAMPLE

Suppose you were asked to give a presentation to upper management to defend the need for your department's request for a 20% budget increase next year. You know it is going to be a persuasive presentation, and you have completed your audience analysis sheet (page 20). You created 10 to 15 original ideas to focus on and have narrowed them down to the following three:

We need to update our computer system	More programmers are needed to develop our systems	We must finance development

These three ideas are the general assertions you plan to make to your audience. Specific explanations, evidence and benefits will become your subpoints.

---

*Post-It is a registered trademark of the 3M Company.

STEP #2 - State the Subpoints

Once you have the main points of your presentation, it is time to develop supporting ideas. These may consist of explanations, data or other evidence to support your main ideas as shown in our example.

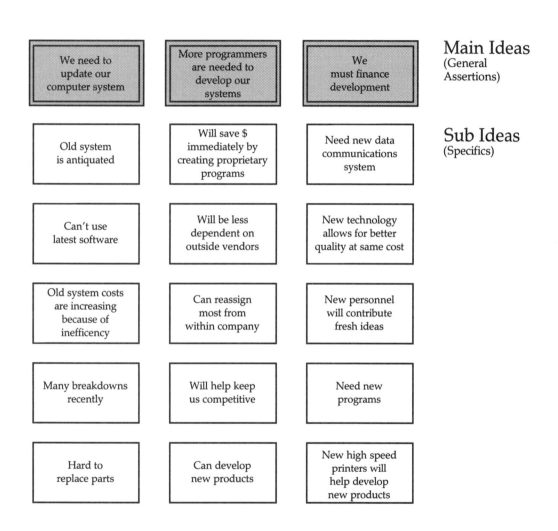

Main Ideas (General Assertions)

Sub Ideas (Specifics)

You may have more or less subpoints in your presentation. Once you have completed this procedure, rearrange your cards to best suit your needs. Try different arrangements to see what will work best. Always keep your objectives and audience in mind.

ORGANIZING YOUR THOUGHTS (Continued)

STEP #3 - State the Benefits

In persuasive presentations, it is necessary to tell the audience *specifically* what benefits they will receive if they do what you ask. Benefits are usually placed in the body of the presentation. An alternate method of organizing a persuasive presentation might be to simply use the benefits as the main points. From the previous example (Why our department needs a 20% larger budget next year) we might summarize the following benefits to our audience:

1. More money in our department will allow for a new computer system that will keep us competitive in our industry.

2. It, along with the necessary programmers, will increase profits because of greater efficiency.

3. A new system will allow us to upgrade our existing products, as well as develop new ones.

STEP #4 - Develop Handouts

Now you can decide what handouts (if any) would add to your presentation. Following are three major uses of handouts in a presentation:

1. To reinforce important information.

2. To summarize action items for the audience to follow up on.

3. To supply supporting data you don't want cluttering your visual aids.

STEP #4 - Develop Handouts (continued)

Once you have decided what handouts would be beneficial you must then decide when you are going to hand them out. There are three alternatives:

BEFORE THE PRESENTATION

The main problem with this is that your audience may wish to satisfy their curiosity about the contents of your handout as you are speaking. When people are reading, they are not listening. One way to deal with this problem is to have the handout in place when the audience enters the room. This will allow them to read it before you begin speaking. In addition, you can explain the handout, satisfying their curiosity about its contents.

DURING THE PRESENTATION

This must be used carefully. Handouts during a presentation must be disbursed quickly and be relevant to the point you are making. Otherwise they will be a distraction, not an aid.

AT THE END OF THE PRESENTATION

During your presentation you can inform the audience that they will receive a handout covering such and such points at the end of your presentation. This will allow them to avoid having to take necessary notes. However, whether or not you use this technique depends on your audience analysis. If the audience is accustomed to receiving handouts with presentations, or if it would be useful for them to follow the presentation with the data before them, you might not want to withhold them. But, if it is going to distract from your verbal presentation (such as glossy photos, marketing brochures, etc.) and not add substantially to the presentation, hold them back.

STEP #5 - Develop Visual Aids

Once your organizational pattern has been established, you need to decide if and where you are going to use visual aids. Guidelines for developing and using visuals in a presentation are discussed later (beginning on page 33). For now it is important only that you determine how they will fit into your plan.

For example, the third subpoint under the first major idea in our sample presentation developed on page 23, states that the old computer system is costing the company money. This point could be illustrated with a graph, or similar visual, showing the cost of the computer over the past three years versus the savings of a new system during the same time span.

ORGANIZING YOUR THOUGHTS (Continued)

> ## STEP #6 - Main Idea Preview/Review Sentence

Have you ever heard the saying:

Tell them what you're going to tell them—

Tell them—

Then tell them what you told them!

In other words, preview and review the main points in your presentation. This can be accomplished very easily by using a main idea preview sentence and a main idea review sentence. These sentences are separate from the introduction and conclusion.

Going back to the three main points in our example which were:

We need to update our computer	More programmers are needed to develop our systems	We must finance development

(Remember our objective is to convince upper management that our department needs a 20% larger budget for the next fiscal year.) The main idea preview sentence then is, *"We need to update our computer system, hire more programmers and finance development for several reasons which I will share with you today."* Before the conclusion you can use a similar sentence to review the main ideas as well; (i.e. *"You have now seen why an updated computer system, adequate staff and budget for new development is a good idea."*)

> **All effective presentations make the pattern of organization crystal clear to the audience.**

STEP #7 - Develop the Introduction

Introductions consist of two major functions:

1. Providing necessary information—This might include background material, establishing the significance of the topic, introducing yourself and establishing your credibility by telling the audience why you're qualified to speak on the topic. You may have additional types of information that would be appropriate to deliver at this point.

2. Getting attention—Right before the presentation the audience may be chatting with one another, daydreaming or reading the handout material that you have cleverly placed on the table in advance of the presentation!

Each presentation situation will call for its own necessary information depending on your audience analysis. However, almost all presentations require some type of attention getter. The smaller the group the smaller the attention getting device. Here are some of the more common types:

Technical Background—

Often speakers have to introduce their topic by giving some background information or data; they need to set the stage for what is to come in the body of the presentation. For example, *"Before discussing some of the formulas for the new compounds I would like to give you a brief overview of our past research."*

Anecdote—

An anecdote is a short story used to help illustrate a point. It is sometimes humorous but not always. An example might be something like this. *"My son came to me the other day and said, 'Dad, if you raise my allowance by $2.00 I'll double mow the lawn each week. For another 10% you will get the best looking lawn in the neighborhood.' In the same way, if we raise salaries for our production workers 10%, we should expect to increase productivity."*

Humor—

Humor is a great way to break the ice. But beware! Humor must be linked to either the speaker, topic, audience or the occasion. Also, never tell a joke that is sexist, racist or makes fun of national origin, religion or any personal topic. If you ask yourself, "Should I tell this joke?" don't!!! Be conservative with your use of humor.

ORGANIZING YOUR THOUGHTS (Continued)

STEP #7 - Develop the Introduction (Continued)

There is nothing worse than a joke used in an introduction that has no connection to the speech (*i.e. "Did you hear about the duck who walked into the store, ordered a lot of items and asked it all to be put on his bill? Well, today I would like to talk about networking off of our mainframe."*). Nothing is more embarrassing than a joke that falls flat.

Involving Question—

There are two ways to do this. First, you can ask an open-ended question, but beware, someone might yell out the wrong answer or crack a joke at your expense. The second way, and the safer of the two, is to ask for a show of hands. It's no guarantee that you won't get heckled but generally audiences will respond the way you request them to.

Rhetorical Question—

A rhetorical question is a question with an obvious answer. An example is, *"How many people here want bigger research grants?"* This device is an excellent way to get the audience's attention.

Shocking Statement—

A statement such as, *"Last year enough people died in automobile accidents to fill every seat in the local university's football stadium. This is why I am going to convince you to wear seatbelts."* This type of statement will help capture your audience's attention.

Quotation—

You may wish to begin your presentation with a *brief* quotation. Quotations should be limited to a sentence or two and the source of the quotation should always be given. It is OK to read a quotation directly since you want it to be accurate. Avoid memorizing all but the simplest or well-known quotes. You may wish to paraphrase a famous quote, possibly something like, "To paraphrase Mark Twain, Everyone complains about the computer system but no one does anything about it!"

STEP #8 - Develop the Conclusion

Good conclusions always return to material in your introduction. They normally should reference the background material, rhetorical question, anecdote or data that you used in your introduction.

In persuasive presentations you sometimes need a ''call-to-action'' statement in your conclusion. Tell your audience what they need to do (i.e. should they call a section meeting to implement that new solution? Should they give you that budget increase?) Your conclusion should tell them what specific action they need to take, how to take it, and when it must be taken.

Introductions and conclusions put the head and tail on the body of your presentation. Without them, or with them not fully developed, you don't have a complete presentation and it will be evident to the audience.

PLANNING AND ORGANIZING YOUR PRESENTATION REVIEW CHECKLIST

(Use this sheet to help prepare your next presentation)

Plan Your Presentation:

For my presentation I have:

☐ Developed Objectives

☐ Analyzed the Audience

Organize Your Presentation:

For this presentation I have:

☐ Brainstormed Main Ideas

☐ Brainstormed Sub Ideas

☐ Developed Handouts

☐ Developed Visual Aids

☐ Stated the Benefits (in persuasive presentations)

☐ Stated the Main Idea Preview/Review Sentence

☐ Structured the Introduction

☐ Developed the Conclusion

P A R T

III

VISUAL AIDS

DEVELOPING AND USING VISUAL AIDS

In this section you will learn how to prepare and use visual aids in your speech. Most presentations in the business and professional world use overhead transparencies, so we will focus on their use. However, tips on using flipcharts, 35mm slides and other media are also covered in this section.

USE VISUAL AIDS WHEN YOU NEED TO:

1. Focus the audience's attention.

2. Reinforce your verbal message (but don't repeat it verbatim!).

3. Stimulate interest.

4. Illustrate factors that are hard to visualize.

5. Graphically represent data.

DON'T USE VISUAL AIDS TO:

1. Impress your audience with overly detailed tables or graphs.

2. Avoid interaction with your audience.

3. Make more than one main point.

4. Present simple ideas that are easily stated verbally.

PLANNING YOUR VISUAL AIDS

10 Tips for Planning Successful Visual Aids

When considering what type of visual representation to use for your data or ideas there are some rules of thumb to consider:

1. **Use visual aids sparingly.** One of the biggest problems in technical presentations is the overuse of visual aids. A useful rule of thumb is one visual aid for every two minutes of presentation time.

2. **Use visual aids pictorially.** Graphs, pictures of equipment, flow charts, etc., all give the viewer an insight that would require many words or columns of numbers.

3. **Present one key point per visual.** Keep the focus of the visual simple and clear. Presenting more than one main idea per visual can seriously detract from the impact.

4. **Make text and numbers legible.** Minimum font size for most room setups is 18 pt. If you are not sure then walk to the back of the room where it will be used, or a similar room, and look at the chart. Can you read everything? If not, be prepared to provide additional explanation in handout material or highlight the areas of the chart where you want the audience to focus.

5. **Use color carefully.** Use no more than 3-4 colors per visual aid to avoid a cluttered rainbow effect. The colors used should contrast with each other to provide maximum visibility, for example, a dark blue background with light yellow letters or numbers. Avoid patterns in color presentations, they quickly become hard to distinguish.

6. **Make visuals big enough to see.** Walk to the last row where people will be sitting and make sure that everything on the visual can be seen clearly.

7. **Graph data.** Whenever possible avoid tabular data in favor of graphs. Graphs allow the viewer to picture the information and data in a way that numbers alone can't do. Consult the information on the following pages on how to graph data.

8. **Make pictures and diagrams easy to see.** Too often pictures and diagrams are difficult to see from a distance. The best way to ascertain this is to view it from the back of the room where the audience will be. Be careful that labels inside the diagrams are legible from the back row also.

9. **Make visuals attractive.** If using color, use high contrast such as yellow on black or yellow on dark blue. Avoid clutter and work for simplicity and clarity.

10. **Avoid miscellaneous visuals.** If something can be stated simply and verbally, such as the title of a presentation, there is no need for a visual aid.

Use the following form to help you plan and visualize the visuals you would like to use in a presentation. The first one is done for you as an example:

Key idea to be expressed.	Visual representation

1. *Signal and frequency are directly related.*

2. _____

3. _____

4. _____

PLANNING YOUR VISUAL AIDS (Continued)

Revelation vs Overlay—

The process of covering part of an overhead transparency and revealing the contents by sliding the cover down is disliked by a considerable portion of the population. There is nothing wrong with this procedure—it's simply a matter of personal preference. However, you never know who in the audience won't like it. So, if possible, avoid it.

The other reason for using overlays rather than revelation is to present complicated graphs or other forms of data in such a fashion that the audience won't be overwhelmed by it. Building the information slowly, as illustrated below, allows time to absorb the information and to more easily see the relationship of the data being presented.

Overlays are simple to produce. On the computer, or other production device, you prepare successive transparencies that, when laid on top of one another, add the information into the chart so that the lines and columns are aligned.

Example of word chart overlays:

Problems With Power Plant Emissions:	Problems With Power Plant Emissions:	Problems With Power Plant Emissions:
1. Health Effects	1. Health Effects	1. Health Effects
	2. Corrosives	2. Corrosives
		3. Transport

Example of layering information for graph overlays:

1st transparency:

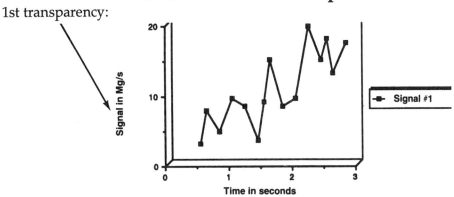

Additional
transparency
overlays

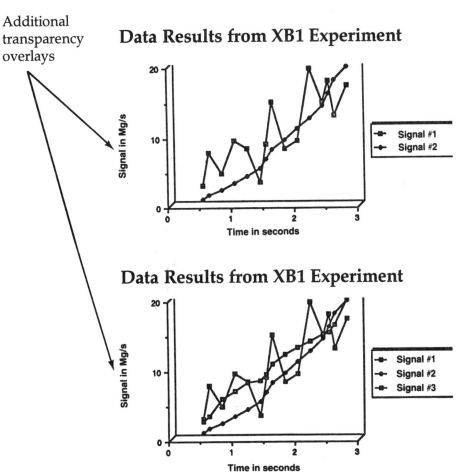

DEVELOPING AND USING VISUAL AIDS
(Continued)

When constructing visual aids employ the K.I.S.S. principle—keep it short and simple! Don't overload charts with too much data. When you do, your audience will quickly lose interest, or get lost.

Avoid charts like this one.

$$\left[1-\frac{u}{u^*}\right]\mathbf{Q}_{d-1}\left[\mathbf{V}_0^{[0]}(u^*),\mathbf{V}_0^{[1]}(u^*),\ldots,\mathbf{V}_0^{[d-1]}(u^*);0,u^*;\frac{u}{u^*}\right]$$

$$+\frac{u}{u^*}\left[u^*\mathbf{Q}_{d-1}\left[\mathbf{V}_1^{[0]}(u^*),\mathbf{V}_1^{[1]}(u^*),\ldots,\mathbf{V}_1^{[d-1]}(u^*);0,u^*;\frac{u}{u^*}\right]\right.$$

$$\left.+(1-u^*)\mathbf{Q}_{d-1}\left[\mathbf{V}_0^{[0]}(u^*),\mathbf{V}_0^{[1]}(u^*),\ldots,\mathbf{V}_0^{[d-1]}(u^*);0,u^*;\frac{u}{u^*}\right]\right]$$

Regrouping, we have

$$\left[1-\frac{u}{u^*}\right]\mathbf{Q}_{d-1}\left[\mathbf{V}_0^{[0]}(u^*),\mathbf{V}_0^{[1]}(u^*),\ldots,\mathbf{V}_0^{[d-1]}(u^*);0,u^*;\frac{u}{u^*}\right]$$

$$+\frac{u}{u^*}\mathbf{Q}_{d-1}\left[(1-u^*)\mathbf{V}_0^{[0]}+u^*\mathbf{V}_1^{[0]}(u^*),\right.$$

$$(1-u^*)\mathbf{V}_0^{[1]}+u^*\mathbf{V}_1^{[1]}(u^*),\ldots,$$

$$\left.(1-u^*)\mathbf{V}_0^{[d-1]}+u^*\mathbf{V}_1^{[d-1]}(u^*);0,u^*;\frac{u}{u^*}\right]$$

By definition (10.12) of $\mathbf{V}_i^{[r]}(u^*)$, this becomes

$$\left[1-\frac{u}{u^*}\right]\mathbf{Q}_{d-1}\left[\mathbf{V}_0^{[0]}(u^*),\mathbf{V}_0^{[1]}(u^*),\ldots,\mathbf{V}_0^{[d-1]}(u^*);0,u^*;\frac{u}{u^*}\right]$$

$$+\frac{u}{u^*}\mathbf{Q}_{d-1}\left[\mathbf{V}_0^{[1]}(u^*),\mathbf{V}_0^{[2]}(u^*),\ldots,\mathbf{V}_0^{[d]}(u^*);0,u^*;\frac{u}{u^*}\right]$$

But from (10.6), this is just

$$\mathbf{Q}_d\left[\mathbf{V}_0^{[0]}(u^*),\mathbf{V}_0^{[1]}(u^*),\ldots,\mathbf{V}_0^{[d]}(u^*);0,u^*;\frac{u}{u^*}\right]$$

Simplify the chart and focus audience attention where you want it.

INFORMATION CONTENT GUIDELINES FOR NUMBER CHARTS

NUMBER CHARTS—**USE A MAXIMUM OF 25-35 NUMBERS PER VISUAL AID.** One number can have many digits so use good judgment if you are not sure. The general rule of thumb is to *put raw data into the handout material or on backup overheads, not on the screen* (unless your boss tells you to do so!). Data charts should only contain bottom line information, conclusions and final results. Another alternative is to graph the data in a visually pleasing manner.

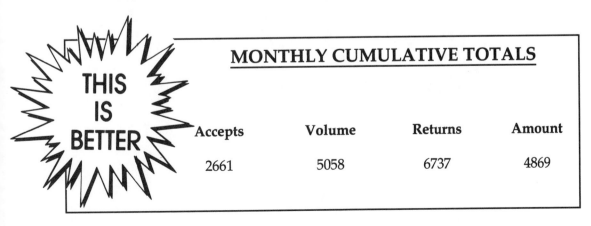

MONTHLY CUMULATIVE TOTALS

	Accepts	Volume	Returns	Amount
	179.880	423.3660	967	334.07
	128.864	345.7670	860	287.74
	34.221	678.4440	733	982.21
	129.775	654.9980	1887	658.89
	378.664	739.6000	431	295.58
	194.775	187.4659	223	295.50
	198.856	189.9570	582	377.89
	746.599	879.9560	334	867.73
	286.675	385.7689	233	286.57
	196.999	285.8678	188	296.97
	185.868	286.8786	299	185.90
Totals:	2661.767	5058.3140	6737	4869.13

In this case, *only the totals line* is essential—the rest of the information *could be put in a handout.*

MONTHLY CUMULATIVE TOTALS

Accepts	Volume	Returns	Amount
2661	5058	6737	4869

40

Avoid "Data Dump". Crowding your presentations with too many visuals and/or too much information will reduce their effectiveness and you will lose impact. Usually the fewer, the better!

INFORMATION CONTENT GUIDELINES FOR WORD CHARTS

FOR WORD CHARTS—**USE A MAXIMUM OF 36 WORDS PER VISUAL AID** (excluding the title). Try to fit your material into a maximum of six lines, with no more than six words per line. If you need more room, (as in the example below), use more lines, but fewer words. There is no need to repeat every word in your presentation. You simply want to reinforce your main ideas to the audience.

HOW TO ORGANIZE YOUR PRESENTATION

It is a good idea to start by developing objectives. Once this is done you need to thoroughly analyze the audience. You must complete these steps before you separately brainstorm the main points and the subpoints of your presentation. If it's a persuasive presentation, then you must also state the benefits. You then gather factual information and prepare a blueprint of your presentation. Also prepare any visual aids, handouts and notes you will need. And don't forget to practice!

This chart is more effective when it is set up as follows:

HOW TO ORGANIZE YOUR PRESENTATION

- Develop Objectives

- Analyze the Audience

- Brainstorm the Main Ideas and the Sub Ideas

- Develop Visuals, Handouts and Notes

- State the Benefits (in a persuasive presentation)

- State Main Idea Preview/Review Sentence

- Structure Introduction and Conclusion

GRAPH AND CHART SELECTION

Graphs and charts are important tools when presenting data. With a well constructed graph or chart you can easily represent complicated data in an easy to understand visual format.

There is a four-step process to successfully choosing the correct graph form:

1. **Idea**—You must decide what specific message you want to convey in the presentation of the data. What point do you specifically want to make? The point you want to make, i.e., the message, should then be translated into your title. On the visual aid planning form, write the key ideas to be expressed. After reading step two and consulting the matrix, draw a visual representation of the type of graph that is appropriate.

2. **Comparison**—What is the nature of the data that you are comparing? Are you looking at **percentages, parts or items** (sales of part A were larger than those of part B), **time** or change over a period of time, **frequency** of distribution within specified categories or are you trying to **correlate** data to see if a relationship between variables exist? All graphs will fall into one or more of these categories.

3. **Format**—Based upon the comparison you use, you may then choose the proper format. The matrix provided on the next page will help you with this task.

4. **Test**—Don't skip this step. Show the graph or chart to a colleague or friend and ask them to give you some feedback on its clarity. What is evident to you may be unclear to others. Test for viewer comprehension.

USE THIS MATRIX TO PICK THE PROPER GRAPH

	Time	Percent	Correlation	Parts	Frequency
Line					
Column					
Dot					
Bar					
Pie					
Graphic					
3D Combines 3 elements					

TO REVIEW:

There are five basic ways to compare data:

- Time

- Percent

- Correlation

- Parts or Items

- Frequency

There are seven basic graph types to display data:

- Line

- Column

- Dot

- Bar

- Pie

- Graphic

- 3D

DEVELOPING VISUAL AIDS (Continued)

Developing Titles for Your Visual Aids

There are three basic types of titles for your visual aids. Choose the one that best suits your needs:

Topic Title—Used when it is not necessary to convey a specific message but only provide information or raw data, as in the example below:

> **Frequency**

Thematic Title—Used to tell the audience what information they should draw from the data presented. An example would be:

> **Frequency and signal strength are interrelated.**

Assertive Title—Used when you want to give the audience your opinion about what conclusion they should draw from the data. It is used most often in persuasive presentations, as in the following example:

> **We should investigate the relationship of frequency and signal strength.**

HINT:

Make your presentation people centered, not media centered. Often presenters will use too many visual aids and put too much on them. While you may need to use visual aids to present your data, remember that interaction and rapport building with the audience is critical. Visual aids alone cannot communicate enthusiasm and make a presentation lively and interesting; your delivery will be the major factor in many situations.

COLOR IN VISUAL AIDS

With the rapid advances in printer technology, color printing is now within the reach of most computer users. This has lead to a great increase in the use of color overhead transparencies generated by the end user rather than by a graphics house or in-house graphics department.

Below you will find some basic principles for using color in visual aids.

1. Match color with the subject and audience. Consider the purpose of the visual aid and who will be viewing it. A blue background, for example, is more conservative than a yellow background. Keep in mind what moods and themes colors can convey:

   • Tranquility can be conveyed by pale colors, greys and pinks.

   • Warmth is best communicated by reds, oranges, pinks or browns.

   • Coolness can be built in by using certain shades of blue, green and grey.

   • Excitement can be shown by using reds and blacks together with some greys.

2. Pick background colors first before choosing text or data colors. Text and data colors should highly contrast with the background for maximum legibility.

3. Colors should not clash—they should have a high degree of harmony.

4. Avoid the rainbow effect and use no more than 3-4 colors.

5. Generally, assign bright colors to the areas that you want to receive the most attention.

6. Keep the color theme consistent in all your slides.

7. Keep the contrast between the background and the text and data strong.

USING VISUAL AIDS IN YOUR PRESENTATION

Case Study

Paul has to give a presentation to his engineering group outlining a major new project he is proposing for the company. He has spent weeks preparing for this 30 minute presentation. This project is important to Paul, and he is very nervous about presenting it.

Paul prepared 75 overhead transparencies for the presentation. Each is crammed with information. As the presentation begins Paul finds that he is spending more time than he thought he would discussing each transparency. His allotted time is going by very quickly. He speeds up his rate of speech, and to finish on time he shows the last 35 transparencies without any discussion.

Case Study

Gene works in a large computer company. He must make a presentation on the past, present and future of the company's R&D budgets to a group of high-ranking department managers. Gene is very anxious to have his presentation go well.

In Gene's 30-minute presentation he will use overhead transparencies, and he has prepared 10 that summarize important information from his written report. Each transparency deals with a single issue, yet has enough information to cover the subject and reinforce the points Gene is trying to make. He knows that a summary of information on his visual aids will provide enough meat for discussion. Gene's philosophy is to make the visual aids work for him, and not let them overwhelm the presentation.

Who do you think was more successful, and why?

_____

_____

_____

_____

USING VISUAL AIDS IN YOUR PRESENTATION (Continued)

DIRECTING YOUR AUDIENCE'S FOCUS

Learn to direct the audience's focus where you want it. When you use visual aids, the audience's focus is divided. To "win them back" you will need to redirect their focus. This is usually done by closing down the visuals, and taking a step or two towards the audience.

Place a check next to the technique(s) that you plan to use in the presentation you give.

I plan to:

☐ Shut off the overhead projector when there is a lengthy explanation about a point transparency and there is no need for the audience to watch the screen. I won't click the machine on and off in a distracting way, but also I won't leave it on so long that they focus on the transparency and not on me.

☐ Turn a flip-chart page when I have finished referring to it. If the flip charts have been prepared in advance, I plan to leave three blank pages between each prepared sheet so my next page won't show until I'm ready for it.

☐ Erase any writing I have on a blackboard for the reasons outlined above. Any information noted by the audience and no longer needed for future reference can be erased.

☐ Break up slide presentations by inserting a black slide at points where an explanation is needed, or when I want to make a transition to another section. This will wake up my audience and help refocus their attention. I will leave some light on in the room, near where I am standing so that I become the focus of attention when the screen goes black.

☐ Show or demonstrate an object by revealing it when it is referred to and then covering it up when it is no longer in use. If the object is not covered, most people will continue looking out of curiosity and may miss some of my presentation.

☐ Avoid passing objects around the audience since this is very distracting. Instead, I will walk into the audience and show the object to everyone briefly and, then, make it available at the end of the session.

> Decide in advance where the audience should focus. Do you want the focus divided between you and the visual aid or do you need their undivided attention?

USING VISUAL AIDS IN YOUR PRESENTATION (Continued)

Placement of Equipment

When using an overhead projector or flipchart it should add, not detract, from your presentation. This can be accomplished by placing the overhead screen or flipchart at a 45 degree angle and slightly to one side of the center of the room. In this way a presenter can occupy the central position and more easily focus the audience's attention on the explanation of the data being displayed.

Figure #1 shows how a room can be set up to maximize audience focus on the speaker. Figure #2 shows the room set up where the speaker is competing for attention with the visuals.

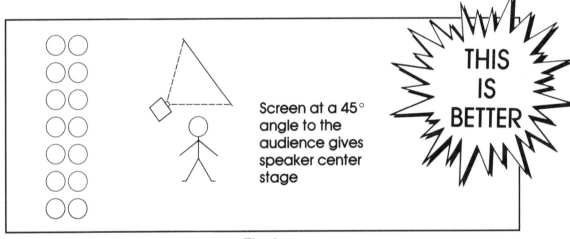

Screen at a 45° angle to the audience gives speaker center stage

THIS IS BETTER

Fig. 1

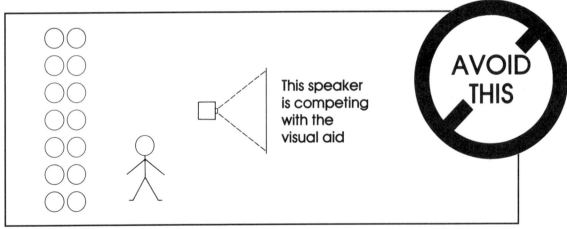

This speaker is competing with the visual aid

AVOID THIS

Fig. 2

Where and How to Stand

One major problem when using visual aids is that speakers often give their presentation to the visuals, and not to the audience. This problem can be easily corrected if the speaker remembers to keep shoulder orientation toward the audience at all times as illustrated in Figure #1. Figure #2 shows what happens when your shoulders turn toward the visuals.

Fig. 1   Fig. 2

Remember: Don't speak until you have eye contact with your audience! If you must write something on the flipchart, overhead or white board, stop talking while you write.

USING VISUAL AIDS IN YOUR PRESENTATION (Continued)

Tips on using a pointer:

1. Pointers should be used to make a *quick* visual reference on a pictorial chart or to trace the relationship of data on a graph. Pointers are not needed on word charts since you can refer to each point by an item or number.

2. When using a pointer, keep your shoulder oriented toward the audience. Do not cross your arm over your body to refer to something on the screen. Instead, hold the pointer in the hand closest to the screen.

3. Don't play with the pointer when not using it. Either fold it up and put it away, or put it down.

4. Use your pointer at the screen, not the overhead projector. Standing at the projector will often block somebody's view of the screen.

5. Leaving the pointer on the overhead projector can focus too much attention on the screen and could detract from the speaker.

6. When using a laser pointer don't try to point with it—rather circle the part of the graph or drawing on which you want the audience to focus. This will help prevent your hands from noticeably trembling. Remember that laser pointers are somewhat of a novelty and that the audience may be focusing on it—so use it sparingly.

SECTION REVIEW: DEVELOPING AND USING VISUALS AIDS

> Check those items you plan to incorporate in your presentation.

I expect to:

☐ Use the KISS* principle when designing visuals and not overload my audience.

☐ Use "key words" or phrases only for my word charts.

☐ Talk to my audience, not to my visual aids.

☐ Place myself at center stage.

☐ Use pointers sparingly and not nervously fiddle with them.

---

*Keep It Short and Simple

P A R T

IV

NEW TECHNOLOGY FOR PRESENTATIONS

NEW TECHNOLOGY FOR PRESENTATIONS

The advances in computer technology have lead to tremendous leaps in presentation technology. You can easily merge photos, sound and video into a presentation on your computer screen and project it directly from the computer onto any size monitor. It won't be long before some presentations will be made using Virtual Reality technology! Here's a brief overview of current technology for creating visual aids and presentations:

Hardware

Computers—Regardless of the type of system that is being used, current technology demands an increasing amount of available memory. If you are considering purchasing a system, it would probably be wise to get the largest amount of internal memory that is available with the system and make sure that extended memory can be expanded later. Some systems require special cards for video or color. Most of the software options discussed in this book come in versions for the various types of computers.

Printers—The price of a good color printer is now very reasonable and should be considered part of the basic system for developing either 35mm slide or overhead presentations. Most of the new color printers provide literally millions of possible color combinations, hundreds of fonts, and can print overhead transparencies directly on the acetate. The new printers have excellent resolution so that visual aids look great.

CD-ROM players—These ''read only'' players (you can't record onto them from your own computer, yet!) can hold a gigantic amount of information. Some disks contain an entire encyclopedia. These devices can store color photographs, video clips, sound clips, huge data bases and other types of information that require a lot of memory. There is new technology available that will allow you to take a photograph, have it transferred to a CD-ROM disk, and then bring it up on your computer screen.

Scanners—Scanners allow you to take a photo or document, digitilize it, and bring it into the computer so that it can be manipulated in any manner desired. Depending on the software that is being used, scanned photos can be placed in documents, on-screen presentations or in visual aids. Scanners are priced about the same as printers and produce images of outstanding quality.

Monitors—Color monitors have grown in quality and dropped in price. Color monitors are useful for composing visual aids that are going to be printed in color. The very large monitors can be used to display a presentation to a group. This allows for very sophisticated presentations which might include video, photographs, sound, etc.

NEW TECHNOLOGY FOR PRESENTATIONS (Continued)

Projection devices—A number of devices on the market allow the computer screen to be projected through the overhead projector onto a projection screen. These devices are less costly than monitors.

Software

There are three basic types of software that are used for production of presentations. Depending upon your needs, budget and time restrictions, these programs can provide you with the simple or the very sophisticated. The three basic types are:

Word processing software—Most word processing programs can be used to prepare overhead transparencies or slide originals. With these programs you can vary font size, present basic data and with some of them include simple drawings and pictures.

Presentation software—These programs are usually very complicated and require some training before they can be fully utilized. However, they are worth the trouble because of the great number of tools they furnish the user. If you are going to be making presentations with visual aids on a frequent basis, these programs are highly recommended.

Most of these programs come with predesigned templates that are visually pleasing and will provide a professional look to your visual aids.

Among the features you will find in these programs:

- Preset formats for overheads and slides called templates. They come in a variety of designs and colors and help the user construct bullet charts, organizational diagrams and other graphic formats. These templates were designed by graphic designers to be visually pleasing and incorporate good color coordination.
- The ability to import graphics and photographs and to then manipulate them to the desired size and area.
- The ability to simultaneously develop visual aids, an outline, notes, handouts and quick switching between them.
- Ready-made format for transfer via modem to a slide production house.
- Spell checker
- The ability to present data in various formats and switch quickly between them to see what looks best.

Graphics software—These programs are usually used in scientific and research environments. They allow the user to create a great variety of graph types, including 3D graphs. Some of them allow for printing poster size graphs for conferences and displays and contain some of the features outlined above.

TELEPHONE AND VIDEO-CONFERENCING

There's no doubt about it, businesses span the globe. There is an ongoing need for communication between employees of the same company who, are working on the same projects, and just happen to do that work half a world away. It is not always practical or possible to get together in person to resolve issues and plan and coordinate details. A letter or memo, even if sent by fax, does not provide any opportunity for immediate interaction and feedback.

This section is designed to help you make ''the next best thing,'' telephone conference calls and video conference sessions, as effective as possible.

Recognize the Advantages and Disadvantages

It helps to acknowledge in advance that a conference call, or even a videoconference, is not the same as a meeting ''in real life.'' Simply acknowledging the limitations and building on the strengths can help the group involved use the tools most effectively.

What are the disadvantages?

Conference Calls: Participants' attention wanders because there is no visual element.

The voice is only an ''involvement'' technique—no opportunity for nonverbal communication.

''Speaker phone'' syndrome—you're never sure who is *really* listening!

Poor phone etiquette—people are impolite because they feel somewhat invisible.

Videoconferences: Equipment is not used to the best advantage. If the camera is preset on wide-angle, and participants have difficulty focusing on who is actually speaking.

Unrealistic expectations of clear communications. Voice activated mikes make two-way communication difficult in some situations.

TELEPHONE AND VIDEO-CONFERENCING (Continued)

What are the advantages?

The advantages for both conference calls and videoconferencing are very similar:

1. **Cost savings:** Many, many thousands of dollars in travel costs can be saved. Business travel is very expensive when you take into account not only airfare, hotel & meals, but also time away from the principal place of work.

2. **Time savings:** A conference call is often taken right at your work station. A videoconference session is held at your principal place of employment, and time away from your desk is minimized. Time limitations, particularly on videoconference equipment, make it essential to keep the meeting moving along in a timely fashion whereas face to face meetings can drag on.

3. **Team work:** While budgets and time may allow for only one or two people to travel to another site, in a conference call or videoconference, larger numbers of people can be involved. Information can be conveyed and clarified on the spot. Conferences can be held more frequently because the cost and time factors are greatly reduced.

Get Ready, Get Set, Go!

The following tips for before, during and after a conference will help you make the most of the tools available. As with ''live presentations,'' the more you practice, the easier it will become. Evaluate and modify your style until you find what works most effectively for your group.

Before:

1. Analyze the audience! Sound familiar? Because you have acknowledged the limitations of conference calls and videoconferences, you need to build a very strong presentation. Talk to people at each site in advance to make sure you are giving them the information they need.

2. Use the Blueprint Form. Again, it is even more important in conference sessions to *be extremely well organized*. Review the section on organizing a presentation, and make sure you follow the technique of preview, develop and review of your main ideas. **K**eep **I**t **S**imple, **S**peaker!

3. Send information out in advance. Make sure all participants have a copy of your agenda, as well as copies of any visual aids you may be using. (Hint: Even in a telephone conference call, if participants have a copy of an effective visual aid, it will help them retain the information being discussed). Again, **KISS!**

4. Make assignments in advance. If participants know what they will be expected to contribute, and prepare in advance, the conference will be much more effective.

5. Be aware of the limitations, and work with them. Keep the presentation lively and to the point; don't get bogged down in endless unnecessary detail. Finally, send the raw data, details, etc., in a handout packet.

6. Develop some ground rules, in advance, to govern question and answer techniques, interruptions and etiquette for the conference.

Specifically for Videoconferences:

1. Familiarize yourself and your group with the equipment in advance. It would be helpful to have a short orientation, even if you have used the equipment before, so that you can familiarize yourself with the controls, how to zoom in, pan, sweep from left to right, where to position the overheads, etc.

2. Arrange for someone other than the meeting facilitator to handle the equipment. Operating the camera and other equipment and participating in the meeting are difficult to do at the same time. Some facilities have a person on site who handles that responsibility. If you aren't so lucky, pick a volunteer!

During:

1. Remember the power of an attention grabbing introduction! After you get your audience's attention, review the agenda, the time schedule and set any ground rules that may be necessary. Review the predetermined procedure for acknowledging and dealing with questions. However you set it up, remember that the ground rules need to be clear to everyone before you begin.

2. Stay with the agenda you have designed. Your agenda needs to be flexible enough to allow time for feedback, but as in a live presentation, some lengthy discussions may have to be taken "off line." Remember the importance of an introduction and conclusion, as well as the preview and review.

TELEPHONE AND VIDEO-CONFERENCING (Continued)

3. Use your voice! In a telephone conference, it is the *only* tool you have, and even in a videoconference, it is essential to keep your voice strong and engaging. Avoid a monotone like the plague, and please, please don't read; talk.

4. Take the temperature of the group periodically. In other words, build time into the agenda to hear from each site and clarify any misinformation. When communicating electronically the chances for mistakes in understanding multiply.

5. Allow time for feedback and commitment to action items at the review stage of the conference call.

Specifically for videoconferences:

1. Be aware of your body! Remember that others can see you, even if you aren't the one talking. If your facility has a third monitor that allows you to preview what you will look like on the screen, take advantage of it.

2. Avoid any side conversations. Because the systems are voice-activated, the picture starts to break up and refocus on another location when it picks up a voice. If you need to have a discussion, use the mute button.

3. Manage audience focus. Keep the presentation lively, and use the equipment to it's best advantage. Judiciously use the zoom to focus on the person speaking. When using visual aids, remember that the graphics need to be bold, simple and to the point, just as they would in a ''live'' presentation. Avoid data dump; crowded or poorly designed visual aids are even more difficult to read from a camera than they are in person.

After:

Follow up! Make sure that the copies of the minutes or action are sent in a timely fashion. Talk to people at the other sites and get their feedback as to how the conference could have been made more effective. Establish a system to check on action items before the next conference.

P A R T

V

PREPARING YOUR PRESENTATION

HOW TO PRACTICE YOUR PRESENTATION

Following is a checklist for your practice sessions. Staying aware of these steps will help you give a more relaxed, confident and enthusiastic presentation.

_____ Make sure your notes are "key words" only. Avoid reading to the audience at all costs. If at all possible, use overhead transparencies or 35mm slides (for large audiences) as "note cards." If you need notes, use *key words only* written in large letters, on a few cards.

_____ Mentally run through the presentation to review each idea in sequence.

_____ Repeat the above procedure until you become familiar with the flow of ideas and where you plan to use visual aids to support them.

_____ Begin stand-up rehearsals of your presentation. Try to arrange a practice room similar to the one in which you will actually give your presentation.

_____ Give a simulated presentation, idea-for-idea (not word-for-word), using all visual aids. Use minimum focus on the notes, maximum focus on the audience.

_____ Practice answers to questions you anticipate from the audience.

_____ Give the full presentation again. If possible, videotape yourself or have a friend give you some feedback.

_____ Review the videotape and/or the friend's feedback and incorporate any necessary changes.

_____ Give one or two dress rehearsals with the presentation in its final form.

CONTROLLING THE PRESENTATION ENVIRONMENT

> **Larry** worked all week preparing for his quarterly presentation. He has rehearsed (standing up and using his visual aids) and feels prepared and confident. The morning of his presentation he arrived early in order to go over his material one final time.
>
> As he enters the meeting room for his presentation, he notices his manager and his department head in the audience. He is anxious but knows he is prepared. He begins his presentation and then moves to the overhead projector to show his first transparency. He flips the switch and nothing happens. He observes that the unit is plugged in. He checks the bulb only to find it's burned out. He knows that most overhead projectors have spare bulbs, but when he looks for it he realizes someone didn't bother to replace it. It takes him 20 minutes to track down a new bulb.

This situation could have been avoided if Larry had checked the projector in advance. A few minutes of planning, checking equipment and arranging seating can prevent disasters. Presenters can usually exercise a degree of control over their speaking environment. Following are eight items to think about before you speak:

1. Overhead Projectors
Make sure that the bulb is not burned out and that there is a spare bulb available. Cleaning the projection screen can sharpen the image. Do you need clear sheets as write-on overlays and pens to use on them?

2. Flip Charts
Is there enough paper? Do you have a supply of marking pens available? Have you checked to insure they have not dried out?

3. Slide Projectors
Is it in working condition? Is the lens large enough to project the image size you need? Does your slide holder fit the projector? Is it located so the image will fit the screen? Does it have a remote switch that works, or can you recruit someone to operate it for you? Have you practiced using the machine?

4. Handouts

Are handouts easily accessible and in order, so they can be handed out with minimum disruption? Have you arranged for assistance in handing them out if needed?

5. Pointers

Will you need a pointer? Is it easily accessible, so you can use it when you need it during the presentation?

6. Microphones

If speaking to more than 50-100 people, you will probably need a microphone. Before your presentation you may want to request a microphone that allows you to move around. You can request a hand-held mike with a 10-15 foot extension cord or a lavelier mike that will hook on your jacket or tie and allow you to keep your hands free.

7. Lighting

Do you need to dim the lights in the room? Check to see if there is a dimmer switch. Having some light on in the room is desirable in 35mm slide presentations, so you won't be a voice in the dark. Check to see that all the bulbs and fixtures in the room are working.

8. Seating Arrangement

If you have control over seating in a room, exercise it. If possible arrange the seating so that the exit and entrance to the room are at the rear. In this way, if people come and go, it will cause the least amount of distraction.

If you know about how many people are going to be present try to control the seating so that there are approximately as many seats as people. This way you won't have your audience sitting in the back of the room. Keeping your audience closer will focus their attention where you want it.

CONTROLLING THE ENVIRONMENT (Continued)

Some possible seating arrangements are listed below:

Theatrical

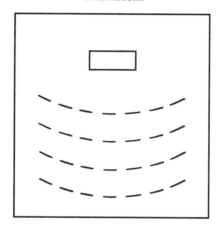

Square

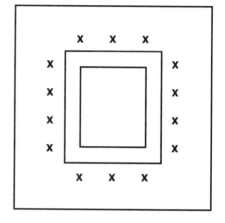

Classroom

Horseshoe

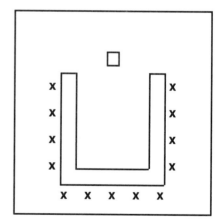

Herringbone

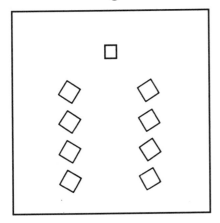

T-Shape

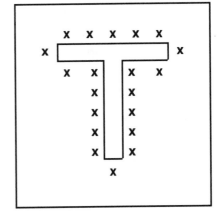

Single Oval or Round

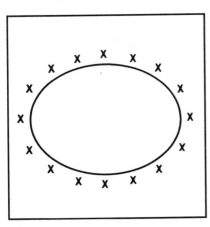

Multiple Round

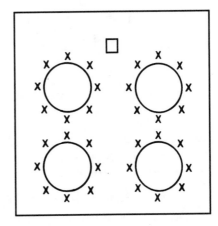

WHEN YOU CAN'T PRACTICE YOUR PRESENTATION— SUCCESSFUL IMPROMPTU SPEAKING

> **Jill** is invited, along with her manager, to attend a meeting of all department heads in the company. She is not expecting to say anything, only to sit and listen. During her manager's presentation, he is asked a question about the department's plans for the coming year. He turns to Jill and says, "Jill, you've been working on our major project for the past year. Maybe you could say a few words about how this project got started, where it stands and where it is going."

If something like this happens to you, don't panic! You already know the fundamentals of organizing your thoughts, and you know your job. With these two resources you can effectively respond by taking the following steps:

Think:

Plug into a pattern of organization.

Any topic can be split up into components. Before you speak break your topic into a pattern such as:

A) past, present and future (or any time-oriented combination);

B) topic 1, 2 and 3 (e.g. production, advertising and marketing);

C) the pro's and con's of an issue (useful in persuasive situations).

In Jill's case above, the time-ordered sequence fits right in.

Then speak:

1. Give a few introductory remarks.

Before you launch into the meat of your topic give yourself time to get collected. Make some general introductory comments, such as, "I'm pleased to be here today to help provide some information. I didn't plan a formal presentation but would be happy to describe the project we've been working on."

2. Develop a clear preview sentence of your main points.

You will want to verbalize to yourself and your audience what your key points are. From the example above Jill could simply state, ''I would like to tell you about how we started this project, where it stands and where we plan to take it''; which is a time ordered sequence.

3. Deliver the body of the presentation.

Talk through each point from your preview sentence. (In Jill's example; past, present and future). Having an organizational pattern established and knowing where you are going will take some of the stress out of the situation.

If what you are speaking about is controversial, first acknowledge the opposition's case but finish with your viewpoint so you end by summarizing your position.

4. Review the main points.

Reinforce the main ideas you've touched upon by briefly restating them. Something like, ''I've tried in these past few minutes to give you an overview of how this project started, where it is now and where we think it will go.''

5. Conclude the presentation.

Don't leave your presentation high and dry. Conclude it with a strong, positive statement. Following our example, ''I hope to attend next month's meeting to report a satisfactory conclusion to our project. I would be happy to take any questions at this time.''

SECTION REVIEW—
PREPARE FOR YOUR PRESENTATION

1. Rehearse your presentation, standing up and using your visual aids.

2. Control the environment by checking:

   • seating arrangements

   • lighting

   • microphones

   • handouts

   • pointers

   • projection equipment, to insure it is available, in working condition, and has the required back-up supplies

3. When you have to give an impromptu presentation:

   • plug into a pattern of organization.

   • give a few introductory remarks.

   • preview and review the main points for your audience.

   • end with a strong conclusion.

P A R T

VI

DELIVERING THE PRESENTATION

HOW TO DELIVER YOUR PRESENTATION

You must communicate your enthusiasm to the audience if you want them to be enthusiastic about the ideas you present.

Standing stiffly, with little animation in your body, and speaking in a monotone voice without good eye contact is a sure way to deliver a speech that is a dud. We communicate with much more than words. Your nonverbal actions carry your feelings. If these channels get cut off because of anxiety, your interaction and rapport with the audience will suffer.

A great benefit of providing an interactive and animated presentation style is that your nervous energy will flow in a positive form and not stay in your body. Seek a natural, conversational style, relate to people in the audience in a direct and personable manner. Even in the most formal situations this is a necessity.

You must learn to be aware of not only what you are saying but also how you are saying it! Learn to be your own coach while you are up in front of the audience, checking the items outlined in this section.

DELIVERING THE PRESENTATION

> ## Deliver Your Presentation in the Following Sequence

1. Introduction

2. Preview sentence (Tell them what you're going to tell them)

3. Main Ideas and Sub Ideas (Tell them)

4. Benefits (In persuasive presentations)

5. Review Sentence (Tell them what you told them)

6. Conclusion

The following tips will help your presentation become animated, interesting and engaging. If you can videotape a rehearsal, watch your delivery. Then rehearse again using some of the techniques described below. Experiment with different presentation styles until you find one that is comfortable and effective.

POSTURE

Keep your posture erect but relaxed. You want to stand up straight but not stiff. Your feet should be pointed at the audience with your weight evenly distributed. Don't place your weight on one hip, then shift to the other and back again. This shifting can distract the audience.

MOVEMENT

Typically, speakers tend to stand in one spot, feet rooted like a tree to the ground. If your presentation will be delivered from a lectern, you should experiment. If appropriate, move to the side or front of the lectern to get nearer the audience. Many professional speakers do this. It is engaging, and audiences feel closer to the speaker without barriers. If you are using a microphone you will need an extension cord or lavelier mike. In a formal presentation, or if the lectern is at a head table, this technique may not be practical.

When not using a lectern, you should normally stay within 4-8 feet of the front row. Don't stay frozen in one spot but don't pace either. An occasional step to either side, or even a half-step toward the audience for emphasis, can enhance your presentation. Stay close, stay direct, and stay involved with your audience.

SHOULDER ORIENTATION

When delivering a presentation, keep your shoulders oriented toward the audience. This will help keep your eye contact on the audience where it should be. Shoulder orientation becomes critical when using visual aids. You will have to angle away from the audience but it should not be more than 45 degrees. DON'T SPEAK UNLESS YOU HAVE EYE CONTACT WITH THE AUDIENCE.

DELIVERING THE PRESENTATION (Continued)

GESTURES

The importance of natural gestures, uninhibited by anxiety, cannot be overstated. Too often anxiety holds back this important channel of communication. We use gestures for emphasis in normal conversation without thinking about what we are doing with our hands. *Learn to gesture in front of an audience exactly as you would if you were having an animated conversation with a friend—nothing more, nothing less.*

Using natural gestures won't distract from a presentation; however, doing one of the following certainly will:

Keeping hands in your pockets-

Or handcuffed behind your back-

Or keeping your arms crossed-

Or in a fig leaf position-

Or wringing your hands nervously-

EYE CONTACT

Interviewing a person who looked at the wall or floor when answering your questions would not inspire your confidence in that person. In our culture we expect good, direct eye contact. Yet in many presentations, a speaker will look at a spot on the back of the wall, or at a screen, or at notes—everywhere but into the eyes of the audience.

Eye contact opens the channel of communication between people. It helps establish and build rapport. It involves the audience in the presentation, and makes the presentation more personable. (This is true even in formal presentations.) Good eye contact between the speaker and audience also helps relax the speaker by connecting the speaker to the audience and reducing the speaker's feeling of isolation.

The rule of thumb for eye contact is *1-3 seconds per person*. Try not to let your eyes dart around the room. Try to focus on one person, not long enough to make that individual feel uncomfortable, but long enough to pull him or her into your presentation. Then move on to another person.

When you give a presentation, don't just look at your audience—*see them*. Seek out individuals, and be aware that you are looking at them.

If the group is too large to look at each individual separately, make eye contact with individuals in different parts of the audience. People sitting near the individuals you select will feel that you are actually looking at them. As the distance between a speaker and audience increases, a larger and larger circle of people will feel your ''eye contact.''

DELIVERING THE PRESENTATION (Continued)

USING YOUR VOICE

There are three main problems associated with voice: a monotone, an inappropriate rate of speech (usually talking too fast) or volume that is too loud or too soft. Make sure your voice is working for you. The following suggestions will help you speak with a strong, clear voice.

Monotone

Most monotone voices are caused by anxiety. As the speaker tightens up, the muscles in the chest and throat become less flexible and air flow is restricted. When this happens, the voice loses its natural animation and a monotone results.

To bring back the natural animation you must relax and release tension. Upper and lower body movement are vital. This doesn't have to be dramatic movement—just enough to loosen the muscles and get you to breathe normally. Videotaping, or audio taping, or feedback from a friend will let you know how you're doing.

> *Learn to listen to yourself; stay aware not only of what you are saying but also how you are saying it.*

Talking too fast.

Our average conversational rate of speech is about 125 words per minute. When we become anxious, that rate will usually increase. An increased rate of speech is not necessarily a problem, if your articulation is good. However, if you are delivering a technical presentation, or one in which the audience needs to take notes, you need to watch your pace.

Another indication that you are talking too fast is when you trip over words. When this happens, slow down. Listen for yourself to say the last word of a sentence, pause where the period would be, and then proceed to your next sentence. Pausing during a presentation can be an effective device to allow your important points to sink in. Don't be afraid to allow periods of silence during your presentations. The audience needs time to digest what you are saying.

Problems with volume.

In most cases, problems with volume can be solved with practice. You need to stay aware of your volume. It is appropriate to ask during an actual presentation, ''Can you hear me in the back?'' The audience will usually be honest because they want to hear what you are saying!

To find out if you have a volume problem before a presentation, ask someone who will give you a straight answer. Ask that person if you can be heard in the back of a room, if you trail off at the end of a sentence, if a lack of volume makes you sound insecure or if you are speaking too loudly.

If your problem is a soft voice, there is a simple exercise to learn how to increase your volume. Recruit two friends to help you. Go into a room that is at least twice the size of the one where you normally give presentations. Have one person sit in the front row, and the other stand against the back wall. Start speaking, and have the person in the back give you a signal when you can be heard clearly. Note your volume level. How does it feel? Check with the person in the front row to make sure you weren't too loud.

A voice consistently too loud sometimes indicates a slight hearing loss. If your voice is judged too loud you may wish to check with your doctor. If you check out OK, then do the above exercise again, but this time let the person in the front row give you a signal to soften your voice, and then check with the person in the back to make sure you can be heard.

QUESTION AND ANSWER TECHNIQUES

HOW TO ENCOURAGE YOUR AUDIENCE TO ASK QUESTIONS

Often you will want your audience to ask questions. When you have delivered technical information, complicated ideas, or are leading a training session, it is a good idea to check audience comprehension by taking questions.

If you ask for questions passively you won't encourage a response. It's mostly a matter of body language. Standing away from the audience, hands stuffed in your pockets, and mumbling ''Any questions?'' does not encourage questions from an audience.

Those who actively seek questions will step toward the audience, raise a hand and ask, ''Does anyone have questions for me?'' You might also ask, ''What questions do you have?'' You *assume* the audience will ask questions, and they often do. Also, pause long enough after asking for questions, so the audience will have time to think of questions (the silence should get to them before it gets to you!). Raising your hand will accomplish two things. One, it is the visual signal for questions and will encourage those who might be shy. Also, it helps keep order. The audience will follow your lead and raise their hands, instead of yelling out their questions.

HOW TO LISTEN TO QUESTIONS

Perhaps you have seen a speaker listen to a question while pacing back and forth, not looking at the question asker, and then interrupt with something like, ''You don't have to finish, I know what you're asking.'' The speaker may not know what is being asked until the question if finished. It is important to wait until the question has been fully asked.

While the question is being asked, you should watch the person who is asking it. Often it is possible to pick up clues to the intensity of the question, the feelings behind it and any hidden agendas if you are aware of body language.

During questions, be careful what you do with your hands! Imagine giving a presentation enthusiastically, and presenting your ideas confidently. Then imagine that when you receive a question, you stand looking at the floor rubbing your hands together nervously. This behavior can negate the confident image you provided during the presentation. Your hands should stay in a neutral position, arms at your sides, fingers open. Focus on the question and listen carefully.

HOW TO ANSWER QUESTIONS

Prepare for questions. You should be able to anticipate most of the questions you receive. Practice answering them. Prepare for the worst and everything else will seem easier. Some speakers prepare back-up visual aids, just to be used when answering anticipated questions.

Clarify. If the question you receive is lengthy, difficult to comprehend, multipart or involved you may want to restate it for clarification. If it is simple and straightforward, this may not be necessary. Very often as people are asking a question they are thinking aloud, and the question might be quite simple but buried in 17 paragraphs of their commentary. Clarification may also allow you to soften hostile language used in the question and it will certainly allow you more time to consider the answer.

Amplify. Have you ever been sitting in the back of an audience and someone in the front row asks a question and you can't hear it? If in doubt you might want to repeat the question so that you are sure everyone heard it. This technique can also give you extra thinking time.

Maintain your style. When answering questions, it is important to maintain the same style and demeanor you used in the presentation. A change in demeanor can suggest that you are not confident about your position.

Be Honest. If you don't know the answer to a question, then you can simply say, "I don't know the answer but I will find out and get back to you." Or, if coworkers might know the answer you can ask them for help.

Involve the whole audience in your answer. Have you seen speakers who get involved with the person who has asked a question and ignore the rest of the audience? In some situations the questioner may try to "hook" the speaker with a difficult question. You can always tell if a speaker is "hooked" because he or she focuses only on the person who asked the question.

QUESTION AND ANSWER TECHNIQUES
(Continued)

Employ the 25%-75% rule. Direct approximately 25% of your eye contact to the person who asked the question and approximately 75% to the rest of the audience. (This is especially important in a hostile question and answer situation). Don't ignore the person who asked the question, but don't ignore the rest of the audience either. This will help you stay in command of the situation and keep the audience involved in your presentation.

Don't preface your answer. Sometimes, when we hear a speaker start an answer with, ''That's a very good question; I'm glad you asked it,'' it may be a sign that the speaker is unsure of the answer.

It's best not to preface answers but simply to go into the answer (after repeating the question, if appropriate). At the end of your question-and-answer session you can say something like, ''Thank you for all your excellent questions.''

Most presentations include time for questions and answers. Sometimes questions are asked during the session and, sometimes, at the end. In many cases a speaker has the option of where he or she would like to have questions asked. If this is the case, then you can ask the audience to interrupt you whenever they have questions, or you can request that they save their questions until you've finished the presentation.

PRESENTATION QUICK CHECK

DELIVERING YOUR PRESENTATION

I plan to:

☐ Stay aware of not only what is said, but how I say it.

☐ Be animated, enthusiastic and direct in my delivery.

☐ Use eye contact to make my presentation personable and conversational.

☐ Keep a clear, strong voice and not speak too fast.

QUESTION-AND-ANSWER TECHNIQUES

I plan to:

☐ Ask for questions by stepping forward with my hand raised.

☐ Anticipate questions and practice the answers.

☐ Watch the questioner and listen carefully to the question.

☐ Keep my hands in a neutral position when listening to questions.

☐ Repeat the question to make sure everyone heard it, or for clarification.

☐ Keep the same style and demeanor that I had during the presentation.

☐ Use eye contact and involve the whole audience in my answer.

PRESENTING A TECHNICAL PAPER AT A PROFESSIONAL MEETING

> **Isaiah** is an engineer about to present the results of some research he has been working on for the past two years. He is making the presentation at a national meeting of his professional society. It is 1:30 in the afternoon and the room is a bit warm. In his 2½ hour presentation he has over 100 slides to show and has little time for breaks since he is planning to read directly from his manuscript. He is worried that the audience will doze off while he is speaking.

Isaiah's worry is well-founded. Reading a manuscript in any presentation can be deadly. At a professional meeting especially, there is the expectation of not only excellent content but a lively presentation of the material as well.

General Hints for Success:

1. Complete the Technical Presentation Check List provided at the end of this section.

2. Plan breaks. Especially after lunch, avoid this time slot if you can. Do not speak for more than one hour without a 5-10 minute break.

3. Rehearse your presentation at least twice. Have a colleague listen to you and throw some questions at you so you can practice answers to questions you might get.

4. Arrive early, check out the room and make sure the AV equipment is in proper working order.

5. Find out if the signals are given or plan a way to watch the time so you stay on schedule.

6. Make sure you have enough handouts for the entire audience and then add 10%, just in case your talk is more popular than you thought it might be.

7. Have fun!

PRESENTING A TECHNICAL PAPER AT A PROFESSIONAL MEETING (Continued)

Organization

A technical presentation and a technical paper are two different things. The paper will tend to be more detail oriented and formal—the presentation will provide more of an overview and be more conversational in its style.

The expectation is that you will be talking *about* the paper—not reading from it. Summarizing the key areas of the paper and discussing them in a professional, but conversational manner, is usually what's called for.

Some of the major areas to be summarized in your presentation might be:

History of the subject or problem addressed

Research approach

Methodology/Techniques

Results

Interpretation

Implications for others

Use Section IV, Organizing Your Presentation, to plan the presentation of your thoughts and data.

Visual Aids

When using visual aids at a professional meeting to help explain your thoughts and data, keep the following points in mind:

1. Avoid tabular data in favor of graphs—this will more quickly allow the audience to see the relationship of the data presented.

2. Avoid ''hand done'' visuals that will detract from the professionalism of your talk.

3. Stick to the information content rules of thumb presented in the chapter on visual aids. Remember the K.I.S.S. principle!

4. Make sure that 35mm slides are placed in a carousel correctly and number them in the lower left hand corner (when held so it reads correctly to you.)

5. Find out how big a room you are presenting in and make sure that the person in the back row can easily see all the material on your visual.

6. Break up slide shows that exceed 20 minutes with black slides that allow for some speaker/audience interaction.

7. Limit the number of visuals—remember the audience wants to hear you present your ideas, not just see your data on the screen.

TECHNICAL PRESENTATION CHECKLIST

Place a checkmark next to...

☐ 1. Complete the Audience Analysis Worksheet in this book.

☐ 2. Secure information on time allotment for presentation and question and answer session.

☐ 3. "Translate" the paper into a presentation format.

☐ 4. If part of a panel presentation, find out what other panelists will present and what time restrictions there will be.

☐ 5. Check on availability, and type of visual aid equipment.

TECHNICAL PRESENTATION CHECKLIST
(Continued)

☐   6.   Plan visual aids.

☐   7.   Produce visual aids.

☐   8.   Rehearse presentation, without reading directly from the paper.

☐   9.   Prepare any handouts.

☐   10.   Plan for breaks during the presentation if longer than one hour.

CHECKLIST REVIEW

EFFECTIVE PRESENTATIONS QUICK REFERENCE CHECK LIST

Check the following items as you prepare and then deliver your presentation.

TO DEAL WITH ANXIETY—I PLAN TO:

☐ Breathe Deeply

☐ Focus on Relaxing

☐ Release Tension by Unobtrusive Isometrics

☐ Move During the Presentation

☐ Maintain Good Eye Contact with the Audience

TO PLAN AND ORGANIZE YOUR PRESENTATION— I WILL:

☐ Develop Objectives

☐ Analyze my Audience

☐ Brainstorm Main Ideas

☐ Brainstorm Sub Ideas

☐ Develop Handouts

☐ Develop Visual Aids

☐ State the Benefits

☐ Incorporate a Main Idea, Preview, and Review Sentence

☐ Structure my Introduction

☐ Develop a Strong Conclusion

TO DEVELOP AND USE VISUAL AIDS, I EXPECT TO:

- ☐ Use the KISS Principal.
- ☐ Choose the Correct Type of Chart.
- ☐ Use Appropriate Titles.
- ☐ Refrain from Talking to the Visual Aids.
- ☐ Place myself at Center Stage.
- ☐ Use my Pointer Sparingly.

TO PREPARE FOR THE PRESENTATION, I WILL:

- ☐ Rehearse standing up and using visuals.
- ☐ Check seating, the AV equipment, all handouts, etc.

WHILE DELIVERING MY PRESENTATION, I PLAN TO:

- ☐ Stay aware of what I'm saying and how I say it.
- ☐ Be animated, enthusiastic and direct.
- ☐ Make my presentation personable and conversational.
- ☐ Use a clear, strong voice.

FOR QUESTION-AND-ANSWER SESSIONS, I PLAN TO:

- ☐ Raise my hand and step towards the audience.
- ☐ Watch and listen to the questioner.
- ☐ Repeat the question if necessary.
- ☐ Maintain my style and demeanor.
- ☐ Answer to the whole audience with my eye contact.

Technical Presentation Skill Workshop

A two-day workshop, 1/2 day seminar and key-note presentation based on the material in this book, and the author's other Fifty-Minute book, Effective Presentation Skills, is available from Steve Mandel. For more information please contact:

> Mandel Communications
> 1425 Hidden Valley Road
> Soquel, CA 95073
> (408) 475-8202

NOTES

NOTES

NOTES

NOTES